STATEMENT

OF THE OBJECTS AND PRINCIPLES OF THE

Yorkshire Church Union.

The YORKSHIRE CHURCH UNION has been called into existence to maintain inviolate the faith of the Church of England, and to promote her welfare and efficiency. Hence, it seeks the attainment of certain objects, and, with the view of accomplishing them, proposes to obtain and spread information bearing upon such objects, as well as to co-operate with other unions of like intentions; and to resist, by all lawful means, every aggression upon the rights, discipline, doctrine, and formularies of the Church, from whatever quarter such aggression may arise.

In carrying out these objects, the Union knows no party but the Church of England, and requires no test which the Church has not authorized. Clergy and lay-communicants are equally invited to join the Union, and have an equal sway over its management.

The Union has put forward the following as the principal objects aimed at by its organization :—

1. GENERAL CHURCH EXTENSION.
2. THE INCREASE OF THE EPISCOPATE IN PROPOR-
TION TO THE WANTS OF THE CHURCH, TOGETHER WITH

THE PRACTICAL ENJOYMENT OF THE SECURITIES, WHICH ARE CONTEMPLATED IN HER FORMULARIES AND CONSTITUTION, AGAINST UNFIT APPOINTMENTS.

3. THE REVIVAL OF A CHURCH LEGISLATURE.

4. THE REMOVAL OF ALL CIVIL IMPEDIMENTS TO THE RIGHT EXERCISE OF SPIRITUAL FUNCTIONS.

All orthodox Christians will allow that general Church extension is imperatively necessary if we would interpose the only effectual barrier against the tide of infidelity, heresy, and schism, which is making such fearful inroads amongst us. In most of the populous parishes of this country Church accommodation and pastoral superintendence are totally inadequate to the wants of the people; while, in many of our rural districts, where such provision is ample, the ignorance or indifference of the people to the teaching of the Church shows that much has yet to be done before the parochial system can be fully developed.

Now, it is manifest, from ecclesiastical history and the present improved condition of our Colonies, that the most effectual means of extending the influence of the Church is to increase the Episcopate—which is the second object of the Union. Common sense, too, suggests, that if our present number of Bishops was considered too small at the time of the Reformation, for a population of about four millions—and that it was so considered is evident from the fact that a provision* was then made for twenty-six additional suffragan Bishops—the same number must be utterly inefficient for a population which has increased more than fourfold! As a Right Reverend Prelate forcibly observes :—

* A.D. 1534. 26 Hen. VIII. c. 14.

"If the Episcopate is to be regarded by our people generally, not merely as a name, but as a living reality, a vital energizing principle—if our Bishops are to identify themselves with their clergy and their people, to throw their hearts and minds into their Dioceses, to be known among their flocks, as St. Paul was among his, to be the friends, the fathers, and the counsellors of their clergy, advising them in their difficulties, arbitrating in differences, peace-makers where their influence can avail, resolving cases of conscience where propounded, forwarding by their counsel every good work and labour of love—if they are to be able to judge with their own eyes as to the practical working of each clergyman in his parish, to strengthen their hands in their hours of trial and perplexity, to encourage the timid and arouse the lukewarm, to let each congregation hear, from time to time, from their own lips, the words of eternal truth, and the poor parents of every parish see that, besides their own appointed minister, there is the chief pastor of the Diocese, who cares for the souls of their children, and is furthering plans for their spiritual benefit—if, I say, these weighty charges really press upon a Bishop, I know not who can be sufficient for these things, according to the present constitution of our Dioceses."—*Bishop of Ripon's Charge*, 1847.

But while the increase of the Episcopate is a thing in itself so desirable, it is, above all things necessary to insist upon the right, (the sole remnant of the ancient privilege of the Christian Laity to guard the Church against the intrusion of improper Bishops,) which, until recently, has never been questioned,* of objecting to the

* Hereford Bishopric Case.

admission into the highest offices of the Church of individuals not duly qualified to fill them, and of having such objections duly investigated and unfit persons excluded. If the various safeguards which the wisdom of the Church has erected against unfit appointments to the Episcopate were deemed necessary in the best and purest ages, how much more are they become so now, when such appointments are virtually made by the Prime Minister of the day, who may be said to be the mouth-piece of that heterogeneous combination of which the State is now composed,—who need not necessarily be a member of the Church, and who may attempt to pervert his power to the spreading of opinions hostile to her teaching. This is an evil, the magnitude of which cannot be exaggerated.

With a view, then, to the attainment of the above stated objects, the Union further proposes to obtain the revival of a Church Legislature, specially suited to our present needs; and, in making this request, nothing is sought for but what is already guaranteed by the laws and constitution of the realm. Magna Charta* expressly provides, " that the Church of England shall be free, and have her rights entire and her liberties inviolate;" and, consequently, that she may herself freely order and settle all things which relate to her polity, and do whatever concerns the settled maintenance of her doctrine and discipline. So deeply and generally felt is the want of a Church Legislature, that the Convocation of the Province of Canterbury, on being assembled with the present Parliament, in its address to the throne, prayed leave to resume its active functions. This address passed both

* A. D. 1215. 17 John.

Houses of Convocation on the 24th day of November, 1817, but in consequence of the death of the late Archbishop, was not presented until the 17th day of June, 1848. No notice has been taken of its prayer by the responsible advisers of her Majesty, notwithstanding the express pledge given in the Royal declaration,* prefixed to the Thirty-nine Articles. "that the Bishops and Clergy, from time to time, in Convocation, upon their humble desire, shall have licence under the broad seal, to deliberate of, and to do all such things as, being made plain by them, and assented unto by us [the Crown], shall concern the settled continuance of the doctrine and discipline of the Church of England now established." The free exercise of this undoubted right is indispensable. No society which has not some competent and acknowledged authority to declare what its principles are, and, when those principles are violated, to vindicate and enforce them, can retain the confidence either of its own members or the respect of those which are without. The Church is a Divine society, and as such has been invested by her Founder "with authority in controversies of Faith†:" and unless this authority be claimed and enforced, the Church cannot be said to exercise her highest functions.

But if the abeyance of such a power be greatly injurious, how incalculable must be the evil which results from the exercise of it by State functionaries. This seems to be our perilous position. The voice of the Church is silenced, and another voice speaks for her a language not consonant with her Prayer Book, Articles, and formularies.

---

* See Prayer Book. † Article xx.

The attainment, however, of these objects would be rendered nugatory without the removal of all civil impediments to the right exercise of spiritual functions. Nothing can be more distressing to the mind of a conscientious parish priest than to minister holy offices to those who, though morally unworthy, have a kind of legal right to receive them. The faithful laity are also scandalized by the indiscriminate use (abuse, it should be called) of our sacred services, which the present want of discipline occasions. At present, the civil power seeks to enforce the ministration of these offices, under heavy pains and penalties, the removal of which is the last prominent object which the Union endeavours to accomplish.

Such, then, are the objects for which the YORKSHIRE CHURCH UNION has been constituted. It need not be added, that there is connected with them the question as to the sort of relation which exists between the Church and the State, and what is the meaning of the term " Royal Supremacy." It is an indisputable fact, that since the time when the Test and Corporation Acts,* and the Acts† which excluded members of the Church of Rome from Parliament, were repealed, the Civil Power has stood in a different relation to the Church from that which it formerly held ; and we cannot but fear that the bonds of that alliance by which it was intended that the Church and State should mutually support and strengthen each other are becoming, year by year, more and more relaxed by the acts of the State.

This change of relation between Church and State

---

* A. D. 1828. 9 Geo. IV. c. 17.   † A. D. 1829. 10 Geo. IV. c. 7.

to which we have alluded, may be discerned from the manner in which, without consulting the Legislative body of the Church, or even allowing it to act, the civil power has altered the Dioceses of our Bishops,—has suppressed ancient foundations in Cathedral Churches,— has forced one person, legally excepted against, into a Bishopric ; and another, against the protest of his own Bishop and the decision of the highest Spiritual Court in the land, into a benefice—has declared that an Article of the Creed is an open question—is secularising the education of the poor—and is now preparing attacks on our Universities. To these grievances may be added the habit, so prevalent in Parliament and elsewhere, of treating the Church as only one of many sects ; and the fact, that in all cases entire freedom of action is allowed to those who dissent from the Church, while the claims and principles of the Church are denied or discountenanced. The attention, therefore, of clergy and laity should be directed to the altered condition of our constitution, because it seems necessarily to require that they should examine the principles on which the relation of Church and State exists, and the distinct and peculiar rights and duties of each. Nor should they neglect such examination, even though it should make it imperative for them to consider minutely what is meant by the supremacy of the Crown, and what are the rights and duties implied by that supremacy.

To effect the objects in view, the efforts of all true Church-of-England-men are required, and these efforts will be most available by each one exerting himself in the station in which he is placed, to make known, by his example and acts, the objects and principles for the promotion of which Church Unions have been formed.

In conclusion, the members of the YORKSHIRE CHURCH UNION humbly hope, that, by the blessing of the Divine Head of the Church, they may be prospered in their endeavours; anyhow they rest assured in the promise that He will never desert His Church, and that those who, in patient perseverance, continue in a right course, will, after enduring to the end, receive from Him a blessing for themselves and for their country.

At a General Meeting of the Union, held at York, January 30, 1851,

It was Resolved:—

"That the above Statement be adopted, and copies forwarded by the Secretaries to all Beneficed Clergy in Yorkshire, Members of Parliament for the Ridings and Boroughs, County Magistrates, and to such other persons as the Committee may think fit."

W. H. Teale, Roystone, Barnsley,
W. Pound, Malton, — General Secretaries.
T. Foljambe, Junr., Wakefield,

ILLINGWORTH AND HICKS, PRINTERS, WAKEFIELD.

The Church Association.

LONDON:

WILLIAM MACINTOSH,

24, Paternoster-row.

1873.

Price Twopence.

AN APOSTOLIC WARNING.

" I CHARGE THEE THEREFORE BEFORE GOD, AND THE LORD JESUS CHRIST, who shall judge the quick and the dead at his appearing, and his kingdom; preach the Word; be instant in season, out of season; reprove, rebuke, exhort, with all long-suffering and doctrine. For the time will come when they will not endure sound doctrine; but after their own lusts shall they heap to themselves teachers, having itching ears; and they shall turn away their ears from the truth, and shall be turned unto fables."—2 TIM. iv. 1—4.

INTRODUCTION.

THE substance of the following pages first appeared in the form of letters addressed to the Editor of *The Isle of Wight Times*. By publishing his sentiments where he is known, with his name attached, the writer hoped that some persons might be induced to read what would be passed over, coming before them anonymously, or under a name expressive of no local interest. He has good reason to believe he was not wrong in his expectation; and is encouraged by the conviction that what has been read, however feebly stated, cannot fail to commend the Church Association to favourable consideration—want of information on the subject was the real want.

Friends, in whose judgment the writer feels much confidence, have persuaded him that the substance of the letters might be adapted to more general usefulness.

There exists, so far as the writer knows, no comprehensive statement of the kind; and therefore, with the hope that the opinion of friends may prove correct, he has recast and enlarged the original letters, and commits them to the press in the present form.

CHARLES A. BURY.

Sandown, Isle of Wight,
March, 1873.

CHAPTER I.

———

ITS ORIGIN.

About the year 1834 there arose in Oxford a new
school of Divines, headed by three men of note in that
University. Each was eminent for his learning, and
all were of high standing. One was a man of great
erudition and high poetic talent; who yet by the qua-
lities of his heart made perhaps a deeper impression on
the wide circle of his acquaintance than the exquisite
poetry of "The Christian Year" has left on the sentiments of the thousands of its readers. JOHN KEBLE has
gone to his rest honoured and beloved of men. The
second is a man of keener intellect, if not equally attractive in disposition; distrusted in the earlier years of
his career; but since the publication of his "Apologia,"
universally felt to be intensely honest—too honest, as
it would seem, for the purposes of the Church to which
he now belongs; for while another seceder, of inferior
intellectual power and literary acquirement—superior
only in astuteness—occupies the Primacy of the Roman
Catholic Church in this country, JOHN HENRY NEWMAN
lingers, almost forgotten, in the obscure shade of the
Birmingham Oratory. The last, but not the least—
nay, *facile princeps*—of the triumvirate retains his
position in his University, and shelters beneath the
skirts of his vast learning the unworthy successors to
the writers of the "Tracts for the Times"—scholars
whose highest literary efforts culminate in elabo-
rate articles on the importance of receiving Holy

Communion fasting, and whose thoughts are stirred by the colour of a stole, or the cut of a chasuble. He who traces these lines retains a grateful recollection of kindness shown him more than forty years ago by DR. EDWARD BOUVERIE PUSEY.

These giants were attended by many of less note, each shining with some brilliancy—among them the two Wilberforces—honoured name! worthy sons of a most worthy father, who did not hesitate to sacrifice station and emolument to their convictions. Many others did likewise: for clergymen were honest in those days ; no Church Association was then needed. When a clergyman found, through change of sentiments, he could no longer creditably retain his position in the Church of England, he left it.

The object proposed by the party was the revival of Church Principles, and the means employed was the publication of tracts explaining and enforcing those principles. The earlier numbers contained little that was reprehensible and much that was to be commended. A certain laxity and disregard for Church order was thought to exist even among those who were most devoted to the work of their Divine Master, and this needed correction.

From the first, however, the Tracts betrayed a Romeward tendency, which aroused the suspicions of some; and the writers soon justified these suspicions by leaving the fountain of truth, the Holy Scriptures, to dabble in the muddy streams of the Fathers. The consequence was, they soon came to substitute the authority of the fathers and of tradition for that of the Word of God.

But though these men did dishonour to God's Word written, they gave no occasion for a Church Association. The work of refutation devolved on riper scholars and better logicians. Argument must be met by argument : logic must encounter logic. A champion for the truth was soon found—one well qualified, of shrewder intellect, and of far deeper research. Dean Goode entered the lists : and his work, "The Rule of Faith," remains to this day unanswered and unanswerable—a rich storehouse of instruction as to the real value of the Fathers, and a still richer exposition of the great truths of inspiration.

"The Tracts for the Times" made a deep impression on the clergy of the day, and influenced many of the highly educated among the laity; but they failed to tell upon the masses, and the impression made was not lasting.

The Tractarians knew too well their duty as citizens to resist authority; and, therefore, created no necessity for a Church Association. When Tract 90 startled English propriety, and disgusted English honesty, the matter was submitted to the judgment of the then Bishop of Oxford, who recommended that the tracts should cease. That recommendation was accepted as authoritative, and acted upon. There appeared no more "Tracts for the Times."

But another generation arose that knew not the learning of Pusey and Keble, or the honesty of Newman and the Wilberforces; though they fain would be accounted the successors of the Tractarians.

Yet were these men wiser in their generation. They knew that most minds receive impressions more readily through the eye and the ear than directly from the brain. Therefore, for argument they substituted show; and in the place of logic they gave sound. They introduced into the services of the English Church rites and ceremonies more or less resembling those of the Church of Rome. Much wisdom was displayed by the leaders of the movement. They did not then, as they do now, boldly avow their intention of unprotestantizing our Church and nation. As time went on, they waxed bolder; and instead of joining a Church which more fully expressed their opinions and reflected their sentiments, they resolved, so far as in them lay, to

bring all Romish doctrines and practices into the
English Church. Aggrieved parishioners appealed to
the Bishops, and called upon them to restrain the innovations. Several of their Lordships, when thus appealed
to, made the attempt in that way which unquestionably
best became their character and office. They gave
fatherly counsel and private admonition; and some
went so far as publicly to denounce the novelties introduced. This gentle treatment proving ineffectual, the
Bishops were then urged to put the law in force against
the recusants. To this they objected on two grounds :—
First, that however repugnant were the innovations
complained of to the plain letter and spirit of the
Articles and Formularies of our Church, such was the
condition of Ecclesiastical law, it was by no means
certain that conviction would follow a prosecution in
the Church Courts; and secondly, that appeal to the
law would involve them in ruinous expenses. These
objections of the Bishops were felt to be reasonable,
and their course was admitted to be most difficult. Those
of them who would have gladly banished from their dioceses these strange doctrines and practices found themselves powerless to do so. The innovating party took
advantage of these difficulties, and advanced more
boldly. What was to be done? It was impossible
justly to cast blame on the Bishops. It was equally in-
expedient to allow our Church services to be remodelled
after mediæval forms and fashions. The straight-
forward course seemed to be to ascertain whether these
innovations were or were not illegal by bringing them
to the test of the law; and if the existing laws should
prove to be so complicated or confused as to be insuffi-
cient for the repression of the evil, then to go to Parliament for a reform of the law; and so render it adequate
to the ends of truth and justice. Now, there was in
existence a Society entitled the English Church Union;
whose object it was to uphold the innovating party and

promote the innovations. If then the evil was to be checked, it became necessary that the loyal members of the Church should combine for the defence of its Protestant character; and the result was the formation of the Church Association. Such an Association had become a necessity: for no bishop or private individual could be reasonably expected to provide funds so large as were required to carry cases through the different courts.

It did not come into existence before it was absolutely required. It was no solitary or doubtful instance of ritual innovation on which its founders acted. The manifest and expressed determination of the innovators was not to rest till their objects were fully gained.

And when they had shown in reiterated instances that no episcopal interference should arrest their progress; and when their defiance of all authority had attained a pitch utterly unintelligible in educated and professedly religious men, then it was that Christian men—men of standing and of good repute, upholders of law and order, lovers of the Church of their fathers, of its simple ritual and its Scriptural doctrines, came forward in its defence, and, with a noble liberality, guaranteed a fund which enabled the Council to take the necessary steps for appealing to the law. They were driven to this: there was no alternative.

It was maintained by the Ritualists that their innovations were according to law; this was denied by the Protestant party—then who was to decide? The questions at issue were of too grave a character, and fraught with too serious consequences, to be allowed to remain in doubt. The Protestantism of our Church was at stake. If, therefore, the Protestant feeling of our people was not to be outraged with impunity; if the loyal sons of the Church of England were not to sit quietly by and see our churches turned into mass-houses, there was nothing for it but to bring the questions at issue before the proper tribunals. The law alone could decide which party was right and which was wrong. Let the authoritative interpreters of the law decide between them. They have decided in very numerous cases; and we owe it to the Church Association that such decisions were obtained. A check was thus imposed on unlawful practices; but it was a lawful check: then what lover of order and justice can blame the Church Association for undertaking lawfully to do that which required to be done; but which there was nobody else to do?

Such is the history of the origin of the Church Association. The disloyalty of the Ritualists to the Church of which they are professed members, and their disregard of episcopal authority rendered its existence a necessity. It has done much good work; but not all that required to be done.

CHAPTER II.

ITS CHARACTER.

The Church Association has suffered much under misapprehension, arising partly through lack of correct information as to its principles and objects, and partly from the misrepresentations of those who love not its Protestant character. The facetious organ of the Ritualistic party, the *Church Times*, has called it "The Persecution Society, Limited." This may be thought to be witty; but is not so really; for genuine wit requires truth for its basis. It may suit the purpose of Mr. Mackonochie and his friends to talk about persecution and martyrdom; but he and others condemned through the instrumentality of the Church Association are no more entitled to be looked upon as martyrs than others who have been found guilty of breaking the law of the land: it matters not whether the law broken has been Common, Statute, or Ecclesiastical law. All subjects of the realm are amenable to its laws; and all men, clergy and laity alike, who wilfully and deliberately break any one of those laws, must pay the penalty. The Clerical offender has no more right to say he is persecuted by those who obtained his conviction, than the most arrant rogue ever placed at the bar of justice can complain of the persecution of the witnesses who gave evidence against him, or of the jury who tried and the judge who condemned him.

Mr. Mackonochie was convicted of illegal practices
—not of the same character, it is true, as those of the
parties with whom he is here classed as a breaker of
the law—but of practices not less illegal or less
injurious to society, though they chance just now to be
fashionable with thoughtless sightseers.

This comparison instituted between the Clerical and
the ordinary offender may probably sound harshly in
the ears of some; but is it a just comparison? If it
be, however invidious it may appear, it is necessary for
the vindication of the Church Association. The true
position of those against whom it has set the law in
motion must be plainly shown. The comparison is not
made to rest on moral or social grounds; it does not
touch the question whether of the two is the more
guilty before God. It compares the offenders simply
as they are regarded by the law of the land, and as the
judges who condemn them must regard them simply as
offenders against the law, and the law knows no dis-
tinction of rank or calling among offenders. Impartial
justice sent Dr. Dodd and Lord George Gordon to the
gallows.

It has indeed been objected in favour of the Clerical
offender, that when he violates the law of the Church
he offends against human law only, while the burglar
breaks one of the Commandments of the Decalogue.
But such an objection cannot be sustained. Even if
the offence committed were no violation of a direct
command of God, the man who deliberately sets at
nought the judicial decisions of properly constituted
authorities, becomes a transgressor of Divine law. If
every soul is to be subject to the higher powers, because
there is no power but of God—either by direct appoint-
ment, or by providential arrangement—whosoever
resisteth the power, whether he be laic or cleric,
resisteth the ordinance of God; and " they that resist

shall receive to themselves damnation." The breaker of a human law which is in conformity with God's Word written is by that same Word brought in guilty before God.

But if the comparison be extended to the consideration of the relative moral delinquency of the respective offenders, what is the result?

Is it correct to say that the convicted Ritualist has broken no divine command? Assuredly it is not. Many of the practices for which Mr. Mackonochie was condemned are idolatrous: the teaching for which Mr. Bennett was brought into Court is idolatrous, and inculcates idolatrous acts. The Church of England teaches that the Romish Mass is " idolatry, to be abhorred of all faithful Christians," and how much less idolatrous are the prostrations of Mr. Mackonochie or the adoration of Mr. Bennett?

If, therefore, the burglar breaks the 8th Commandment of the Decalogue, Messrs. Mackonochie and Bennett have as certainly broken the 2nd. It is in vain, then, to say that the Ritualist is the less morally guilty. Nay, is he not really by much the more guilty of the two? The burglar, when breaking the 8th Commandment, perhaps hardly knows of its existence. In the ignorance of nature, untaught and uncared for in youth, led astray in early life by those more wicked than himself, he knows not God or his laws: in his ignorance and recklessness he has embraced a course of daring against his country's laws, and is at length detected and convicted.

But the Ritualist is an educated man; he has been trained in the knowledge of God's ways; and has become a teacher of God's Word; he knows the strictness of the Divine law and God's hatred of all sin, and especially of idolatry; and yet he wilfully, deliberately, and persistently, with little temptation, breaks the laws of the land, and cannot be ignorant that at the same time he violates a Divine Commandment, and sins grievously against God!

His are sins against knowledge: he is in the position of the servant who knew his Lord's will: and in proportion to his knowledge and intelligence is the measure of his guilt.

And further: he not only himself breaks the Commandment; but "teaches men so": therefore shall he receive the severer condemnation.

But again: it has been pleaded in palliation, the Ritualists are sincere and act conscientiously. It may be so: it is not for us to judge too nicely, however adverse appearances may be. But such a plea is scarcely admissible. Some of the foulest crimes the world has witnessed were committed conscientiously. Our Lord warned His disciples that they would be exposed to the violence of unenlightened consciences, and said nothing in extenuation of the offences so committed.

Neither is the plea admissible before an earthly tribunal: the rebel is not the less amenable to his country's laws because he sincerely believes his rebellion will promote his country's good.

And can men thus guilty before God and man with any show of decency proclaim themselves to be martyrs? or denounce as a persecuting society those who have brought their evil deeds to the test of the law? As well, I repeat, and quite as reasonably, might the convicted burglar give utterance to the same plea.

But it may be said, the Church Association prosecuted Mr. Bennett for opinions, not practices; and surely that was persecution! Now, however warmly we may advocate freedom of thought and freedom of opinion, freedom must have limits, or it becomes licence. We are privileged to live in a free country—the freest land on the face of the earth. All of us have perfect freedom to think and to do all that is right and good. Nay, if so inclined, we may think evil, so far as human law is concerned; but that law will not allow us to publish our evil thoughts if they are calculated to injure our neighbour in his person, his property, or his reputation. Now, Mr. Bennett published opinions calculated in the judgment of many to do serious injury to others. In the first edition of a pamphlet, entitled "A Plea for Toleration," he applied language to the Sacrament of the Lord's Supper not only utterly abhorrent from the doctrine of the Church to which he professedly belongs and whose bread he eats, but such as no intelligent Roman Catholic would subscribe to. But, evidently conscious that he had transgressed the law, and in wholesome dread of the Church Association, he, with the help of one of keener intellect, manipulated the formula of the preceding edition, substituting in the place of *visible* the word *objective*—a word seldom understood by either cleric or laic, and, as thus applied, utterly unintelligible to ordinary minds. So that when the case came before the Committee of the Privy Council, the Judges considered the word so ambiguous that while they characterized Mr. Bennett's language on this and other points as "rash and ill-judged, and perilously near a violation of the law," they gave him the benefit of the doubt, as they were bound to do in a case that was "highly penal" as to whether his words did necessarily express what his supporters and opponents know full well he intended them to express. Mr. Bennett, therefore, was acquitted, because the offence was not proved. Had the language of the first edition of "A Plea for Toleration" been retained, Mr. Bennett must have been condemned, the Dean of Arches being witness; but that language was not before the Judges of the Final Court of Appeal. They put the most favourable construction possible on the words in dispute, and showed an amiable ingenuity in finding a meaning for them which would allow of the acquittal of the accused ; or rather, perhaps, they declined to see the meaning that would oblige them to condemn him.

Mr. Bennett, therefore, was not prosecuted for opinions he held, but for teachings he published to the serious injury of others. He was acquitted, it is true, on the Scotch verdict of not proven ; but none who read with unprejudiced mind the Judgment of the Privy Council will condemn as persecutors that Association which brought to the test of the law published opinions utterly contrarient to the doctrine of the Church of England, and which the Judges themselves were obliged to censure. In no true sense can either Mr. Bennett or Mr. Mackonochie be said to have been persecuted. The latter was convicted of violation of the law, and the term persecution can in no way be applicable to the legal treatment of a convicted law-breaker. The former escaped conviction by substituting for his original statement—without retractation, be it remembered—words so indefinite that even long experienced and able Judges would not pronounce positively and judicially on their meaning. But who does not know—will Mr. Bennett himself deny ?—that the language of the first edition of his pamphlet expressed his real opinions and the doctrines he and his followers continue to preach so far as they understand their own meaning ? As he was not convicted, and did not appear in person or by counsel to meet the charge, he was put neither to trouble nor expense by his opinions being brought under judicial examination. No reasonable person, therefore, even with the aid of the most powerful microscope, could find persecution in the case. If Mr. Bennett thought the doctrine of his Church to be untrue, it was open to him without let or hindrance to join another Church which holds and teaches substantially his doctrine of the Sacrament of the Lord's Supper ; but it is not open to him as an honest man to import into the Church of England any doctrine contrarient to its Rubrics or its known and acknowledged doctrinal standards—much less that especial error in opposition to which the fathers of our Reformed and Protestant Church laid down their lives. The character of the Church Association is that of an upholder of the majesty of the law. Certain men, it matters not that they were clerics and their offences ecclesiastical, conspired to break the law; other men—upright, God-fearing, law-respecting men—combined to vindicate the law; just as we sometimes see done on a smaller scale, by the residents of a neighbourhood for the protection of their property and the prosecution of depredators.

The Church Association, therefore, is not a " Persecution Society." It is set for the defence of the Protestantism of the Church of England, though in the maintenance of its defensive character it has been obliged to assume an aggressive policy in its appeals to the law of the land. Granted that the responsibility of its members is " limited:" the limits they have assigned to themselves are the maintenance of Scripture truth and the protection of themselves and their fellow-Protestants in the continued enjoyment of the doctrines and ceremonies of their beloved Church.

CHAPTER III.

ITS PAST.

THE Past of the Church Association comprises the history of the work it has done. This will be thought much or little according to our estimate of Protestant Principles. If it seem to us a small matter that our country drift from her moorings, and lose her high position as defender of the true Faith; if we are content to see the family of our beloved Queen forfeit its title to the throne of these realms; if we care not that confusion and anarchy take the place of our present happy Constitution, based on the Bible and upheld by sound laws; then may we sit quietly by, and allow to be banished from Church and State every remaining vestige of their Protestantism. If we can look on in unconcern while religion and education are divorced; and the disastrous apathy of some prelates and the ill-concealed sympathies of others, allow a noisy, boisterous, and arrogant party among the clergy to undermine the very foundations of our Church, and drive her loyal sons to seek in disestablishment what may give them more individual liberty, but will assuredly plunge our people into a confused sea of irreligion, Popery, and Infidelity; then will it be to us matter of indifference whether the work done by the Church Association be much or little, useful or superfluous.

But if, on the other hand, we recognise in our Protestantism the source of all our greatness, moral, intellectual, and material; if we are persuaded that our maintenance of the religion of the Bible has secured to us the blessing of Heaven and the consequent prosperity of our people; if we individually have learned to prize the Word of God as our choicest good, and to love that Church which in her Articles of Religion holds forth the Word of Life in its truth and beauty; and in her decent services and admirable Liturgy gives full scope and expression to all Christian sentiment; if we would cherish our country's glory as a Protestant kingdom, and preserve her from partaking in the plagues denounced on the kingdom of the Apocalyptic Beast; then shall we think highly of what the Church Association has done; then shall we thankfully acknowledge that in every instance of successful vindication of the simple rites and ceremonies of our Church, and defence of her Scriptural doctrines, no unimportant victory has been gained for the cause of truth.

In what, then, has the work of the Church Association consisted? What did it propose to itself at its formation, and how far has it been faithful to its professions, and carried out its original intentions?

The Church Association was instituted in 1865; and its objects as decided at its institution are:—" To uphold the Doctrines, Principles, and Order of the United Church of England and Ireland, and to counteract the efforts now being made to pervert her teaching on essential points of the Christian faith, or assimilate her services to those of the Church of Rome, and further to encourage concerted action for the advancement and progress of spiritual Religion."

To these several objects, all concentrating in one point,—the advancement of the kingdom of our Lord and Saviour Jesus Christ, the Council have faithfully, energetically, and in a spirit of prayer, given their best and unremitting attention.

Circumstances decided the special direction of their efforts,—not that indeed most congenial with their

feelings as Christian men ; but that imperatively de-
manded by the proceedings of the Ritualists.

Appeal to the law was forced on them by the denial
that the innovated rites and ceremonies were illegal.

To check the spread of Romish doctrines and practices within our Church was deemed essential to the
promotion of the ultimate object—" the advancement
and progress of spiritual Religion ; " and therefore
notorious offenders were selected, on whose doings the
law was to be set in motion.

The results of the Mackonochie and Purchas cases
are shown in the following statement from the Church
Association Tract, No. 9 :—

ABSTRACT OF POINTS DECIDED IN THE ECCLESIASTICAL COURTS.

IN THE " ST. ALBAN'S CASE."

Martin v. *Mackonochie.*

Mr. Mackonochie was charged with the following
four offences against the laws ecclesiastical, on all of
which the Court pronounced his practices to be illegal.

1. The elevation during or after the Prayer of Consecration in the Order of the Administration of
   the Holy Communion of the paten and cup; and
   the kneeling or prostrating himself before the
   consecrated elements.

2. Using lighted candles on the Communion-table
   during the celebration of the Holy Communion,
   when such candles were not wanted for the
   purpose of giving light.

3. Using incense in the celebration of the Holy Communion.

4. Mixing water with the wine used in the administration of the Holy Communion, during the celebration of the Communion.

IN THE "PURCHAS CASE."

Elphinstone afterwards Hebbert v. *Purchas.*

Mr. Purchas was charged with wearing vestments and adopting ceremonies, all of which, as noted below, were pronounced illegal by the Court.

Vestments.

5. Cope at Morning or Evening Prayer.
6. Albs with patches called Apparels.
7. Tippets of a circular form.
8. Stoles, whether black, white, or coloured.
9. Dalmatics at the Communion Service.
10. Maniples worn by the Ministers.
11. The Chasuble at the Communion Service.
12. Tunics or Tunicles at the Communion Service.
13. Albs.

Ceremonies.

14. Ceremonial mixing water with the wine at the Holy Communion.
15. The Administration of Wine with which Water has been mixed previous to the Service.
16. The administration of Wafer Bread at the Holy Communion.
17. Elevating the paten and cup during the Prayer of Consecration.
18. Kneeling and prostration during the Prayer of Consecration.
19. The use of sanctus and sacring bells rung during the Prayer of Consecration.
20. Agnus Dei, sung after the Prayer of Consecration and before the Communion of the people.
21. Sign of the Cross, made by the Minister at the Apostles' and Nicene Creeds, Absolution in the Communion Service, giving of Sacrament to the people, Benediction, mixing the Chalice in the Service, Prayer of Consecration.

22. Kissing the Gospel Book before reading the Gospel.

23. Standing with back to the people and elevating the cup while reading the Prayer for the Church Militant.

24. Elevation of the Offertory Alms, and removing them to the Credence table instead of suffering them to remain on the Holy Table.

25. Leaving the Holy Table uncovered on Good Friday.

26. Standing in front of the Holy Table with back to the people while reading the Prayer of Consecration.

27. Standing in front of the middle of the Holy Table with back to the people, while reading the Collects next before the Epistle.

28. Standing at the foot of the Holy Table with back to the people, while reading the Collects after Creed at Evening Prayer.

29. Standing with back to the people, while reading the Epistle.

30. Gospeller attended by Acolytes and a Crucifer with Crucifix, while reading the Gospel.

31. Te Deum, sung at the Communion Table, immediately after Evening Service, with Crucifix and banners about the minister.

32. A Procession, immediately before or after Service, singing a hymn, and composed of—Thurifer, carrying and swinging incense : Crucifer, with Crucifix; Acolytes, with lighted candles; Deacons or others with banners ; Choristers, dressed in red and white ; Ceremoniarius, in cassock and cotta, with blue tippet ; Rulers of the Choir, in copes ; Clergy, in copes.

33. Palms, Lighted Candles, and Crucifix, carried in procession at and as a Ceremony connected with Divine Service.

34. Blessing of Palms and giving them to the people during Divine Service on Palm Sunday.

35. Blessing of Candles and giving them to the people during Divine Service on the day of the Purification of the Virgin Mary (Candlemas Day), Ashes on Ash Wednesday, and Palms on Palm Sunday.

36. Candles lighted when not wanted for the purpose of giving light, and used in any of the ways following, during Divine Service,—Carried on Candlemas Day and Whitsun-Day; used at reading of the Gospel; placed on the Communion Table or on a ledge over it, and seeming to be part of it, or about or before the Communion Table, either during the Communion Service or other parts of the Morning Service; Paschal light at Easter.

37. Incense, used for censing persons or things or burnt ceremonially, in or immediately before Divine Service and as subsidiary thereto.

38. Notices of High Celebrations and of Feasts not directed by the church to be observed.

39. Notice of Mortuary Celebration—and Interpolation while reading the Communion Service, after the Collect for the Queen, of a Prayer, Epistle, and Gospel, not in the Prayer Book, read at a Mortuary Celebration.

40. Admission of a Choir Boy, with certain ceremonies, immediately before Service.

41. Metal Crucifix, not part of architectural decorations, on or in apparent connection with the Holy Table, and seeming to be part of its furniture, covered and uncovered ceremonially and bowed to by the Minister.

42. Censing the Crucifix.

43. Figure of the Infant Saviour with lilies over the credence-table at Christmas.

44. Stuffed Dove over the Holy Table on Whitsun-
    Day.

Such is the long list of innovations introduced into
the services of our Reformed Protestant Church by
two clergymen, and now, through the instrumentality
of the Church Association, condemned as illegal by the
Ecclesiastical Courts. But what a sadly humiliating
fact—humiliating to the entire body of the English
clergy—here meets us, that there should be found
among their number men so disloyal to their Church,
so lost to all sense of propriety, that after legal condemnation had been pronounced, they could persist,
the one by evasion, and the other in open contempt and
defiance, in the use of some of these illegal rites
and ceremonies! No marvel that the Lord Chancellor should have uttered so severe though dignified a
rebuke, when, in passing judgment, he said, " Mr.
Mackonochie must be reminded that the right of the
Church of England to ordain ceremonies is asserted by
the 34th of the Articles of Religion, to which he has
given his assent, and that none of the ceremonies which
he practises are prescribed by the Church." Whether
it was certainly known previously that these innovations were contrary to law, perhaps may be doubted,
at least by some persons and in some instances ; but
that they were known by these clergymen to be opposed
to the spirit and principles of that Church wherein they
were privileged to minister, does not admit of doubt.
Time was, when " clergyman " and " man of honour "
were accounted as synonymous terms ; and seldom has a
clergyman been found capable of damaging his name
and profession by deviation from the strictest rule of
right.

Surely the Church Association has not laboured in
vain if it has exposed to the British public the character of these men. Its work done is not to be
restricted to the having brought to the proof the

illegality of forty-four innovated practices. The exposure of the disloyalty of these men to both Church and State, and of their low moral standard, is a most important part of the work. As trustworthy guides and religious teachers, their character is irreparably damaged. These "most conscientious of all men," Bishop Wilberforce being witness, have forfeited all claim to our confidence and respect.

But another and a more important case has been brought into the Ecclesiastical Courts by the Church Association. The cases of Messrs. Mackonochie and Purchas were merely Ritual cases: in them practices only were brought to the test of the law. It was important to establish the illegality of these practices, because innovation of no kind is allowable; and, further, because these innovated rites and ceremonies were said to symbolize doctrines. The precise nature of these doctrines are little known by the laity, and only cared for by the more devout among them. But Mr. Bennett was prosecuted for teaching and publishing erroneous doctrines.

The main issues were the following :—

1. The actual and true presence of our Lord under the forms of bread and wine upon the altar.

2. The visible presence of our Lord upon the altar.

3. The sacrifice or offering of Christ by the priest in the bread and wine.

4. The adoration of the consecrated elements, and the adoration of Christ in the elements.

In the Bennett case, it is true, the Church Association was not wholly successful, but it was essentially so, because the Judgment affirmed the Protestant interpretation of our Communion Service. The condemnation of Mr. Bennett was only a secondary object; the prime object was to establish the doctrine of our Church, and that has been done. Mr. Bennett escaped condemnation—but how? By substituting an ambi-

guous formula for the plain heresy of the first edition
of his pamphlet. Mr. Bennett's real doctrine, therefore, was not before the Court. Had he plainly con-
fessed the real doctrine he taught and still teaches, he
must have been condemned, even Sir R. Phillimore
being judge.

The Bishop of St. David's has expressed an opinion
that " the legal condemnation could only have weakened
the force of the moral sentence in which both Courts
entirely concurred." We cannot agree with this judgment of the learned Bishop :—1st, because moral force
fails to operate in the minds of these men ; and secondly,
because Mr. Bennett and his followers do not confine
themselves in their teaching to the ambiguous language
of the pamphlet. They continue to teach all Romish
doctrine, and are content to occupy the position of
" tolerated heretics."

" It was quite to be expected," again says Bishop
Thirlwall, " that the person whose language had given
occasion to the proceedings should scornfully repudiate
the authority of a tribunal constituted only according
to the law of the land, and not according to his own
opinions and wishes." The severe rebukes of a Lord
Chancellor sit lightly on such as deem themselves to
stand in relation to their fellow-men in the place of
God. The members of the Church Association, however, may feel satisfied that though all was not obtained
in the Bennett case that was desirable, yet in the
vindication of the Protestant interpretation of the Communion Service, and in establishing the legal position
of the Evangelical body in relation to that service,
good and important work has been done.

But if the results of these necessary appeals to the
law are the most conspicuous fruits of the wisdom and
energy of the Council, it may be doubted whether they
are the most valuable. There are often indirect
results of a right and wise proceeding which tell more

effectually on the ultimate issue than the direct bene-
fits manifestly and at once obtained. Such, perhaps, in
this instance, may be considered the check put upon
the Ritualistic movements by the known existence of
such an organisation as the Church Association. If no
such Society had existed, who shall say whereunto
these things might by this time have grown? There
is no other efficient check to their proceedings. Episcopal authority is set at nought by Ritualistic clergy;
and so long as their churches are filled with idle sightseers, they will flatter themselves that public opinion
is with them. Therefore, great as are their extrava-
gancies, many and flagrant as are their breaches of the
laws ecclesiastical, bold, boastful, and defiant as is the
language of the leaders and public organs, how much
worse, who shall say, might have been the state of
things but for the wholesome dread of the powerful
interference of the Church Association! If the older
men amongst them had been restrained by some linger-
ing sense of propriety, there are young men, such as
are described in the charge of the Bishop of Peter-
borough, who feel themselves at liberty to introduce
into the services of our Church whatever occurs to
their own mind.

But the Church Association has done further work,
good, important, and very seasonable work; though it
may not be possible to estimate even approximately the
amount of fruit that work has borne.

Meetings and conferences have been held under its
auspices; lectures many and able have been delivered
by its officers and others; books, pamphlets, and papers
innumerable on Scriptural subjects have been circu-
lated; and so has been disseminated through the length
and breath of our land a vast amount of information
on the principles of the Church of England and of
Protestantism; and who shall say how many sincere
and earnest inquirers after truth have had their minds

enlightened by these means, their hearts warmed towards the Church of their fathers ; and so have become more intelligent and more resolute Churchmen and Protestants. And who shall say to what extent the progress of Romanism and Infidelity has been checked by the promulgation of Scripture truth through the agency of the Church Association! The day alone shall disclose the amount of good that has been effected by the labours of its Council and officers.

Neither must be omitted from the catalogue of works done another advantage that has resulted indirectly, though it is a special object contemplated by the original promoters of the Church Association. Bishop Ellicott has remarked on the closer drawing together, of late, of the Evangelical body. This has been effected mainly through the instrumentality of the Association. The ventilation of the questions it has raised has stirred the hearts of right-minded clergy and laity. The essential points on which true Christians are agreed have assumed more nearly their real importance ; while the minor points of difference have dwindled into something nearer their true insignificance in the presence of a common danger ; and the Church Association has proved a rallying point for good men and true, and a common platform of discussion and explanation.

CHAPTER IV.

ITS PRESENT.

It is quite possible that some persons, though friendly to the Church Association, may doubt the expediency of its continued existence. That such a Society was, in the first instance, a necessity, they are well assured; for they know that it has proved the great obstacle to the progress of Ritualism. But for the wholesome dread which it inspired, we might, by this time, have had introduced into the services of our Christian Church the rites of Paganism itself. But for the Church Association the innovated ceremonies could not have been proved illegal. But for the Church Association we should have had no authoritative declaration of the Protestant doctrine of our Communion service. The Church Association has, therefore, done most important service. But is there anything more for it to do, or that it can do?

Now, it might reasonably have been expected of honest men that when Ritualistic practices had been pronounced by competent authority to be illegal, those practices would, for the future, have been refrained from. When the use of incense, of gorgeous vestments, and lighted candles, was authoritatively pronounced inadmissable to the services of the Church of England, they who considered such things of vital moment should have seceded to a Church which sanctions their use; and they who deemed them only of secondary importance, and not essential to Christian worship, should for conscience and example sake have relinquished their use and yielded a ready, if not cheerful obedience to the law. Neither the one course nor the other was adopted; the Ritualists, as a party, have set the law and its administrators at defiance. These men, whom he who rules the diocese of Winchester once pronounced in his place in Parliament, "the most conscientious men in the land"—and possibly they were as conscientious as other men at that time, before the casuistry of the leaders had blunted the moral sense of their followers —these men, who, when they received ordination at the hands of a Protestant bishop, promised before God, and in the face of the congregation then present, to banish and drive away all strange doctrine; that is, all doctrine opposed to the Articles and Formularies of the Reformed Church, to which they were then admitted as ministers; these pre-eminently conscientious men, a Bishop being witness, boldly avow their intention to unprotestantize their Church, and persist in the use of mediæval rites and ceremonies in open and deliberate contravention of the declared law of the land. This, no doubt, is strange conduct on the part of professedly Christian men. But it is simply the fact; and without attempting to explain, what indeed seems inexplicable, how men professing godliness can thus "resist the ordinance of God," the Church Association has simply to deal with the fact of their persistent use of illegal rites and ceremonies.

Now, if the Church Association was necessary for the obtaining the right interpretation of the law when it was held to be doubtful, it must be at least equally necessary for the vindication of the law now that it has been authoritatively laid down. If the Ritualists persist in the use of ceremonies and in the exercise of practices that have been judicially pronounced illegal, there should be ready at hand some instrumentality competent to bring upon them the penalty incurred. There is nothing save the Church Association that can keep them in check. These men, who once professed an almost abject submission to Episcopal rule, now write of and to the Bishops with a flippancy as offensive to good taste, as opposed to morality and religion. The continued existence, therefore, of the Church Association is a necessity as a standing check to the unlawful deeds of these men.

But further: it was hoped that when the law was clearly defined, the Bishops would not hesitate to carry it out. It is difficult to account for the apparent inertness of the Episcopal Bench. It seems hardly possible that they can expect these men to act more wisely, with greater moderation, and in obedience to the law, so long as they are left to themselves. There certainly are no symptoms of such improvement. On the contrary, year after year, nay, month after month, they introduce fresh novelties; and week after week the language of their public organs becomes more insolent, more boastful, and more defiant.

It is not for us to judge those in authority. To their own Master they stand or fall. But it is impossible not to regret most deeply the present inactivity of the Bishops, and to dread its consequences to themselves and to the Church. We have to do only with the fact that the Episcopal Bench does not act with the decision which is essential and seems to be comparatively easy. And that fact establishes an additional necessity for the continued existence of the Church Association.

These conscientious men, Mr. Bennett and the extreme men of his party, are content to hold and to teach what they know, or ought to know, to be contrary to the doctrine of the Church in which they minister. This, in the eyes of truth-loving Englishmen, is not seemly. Convicted at the bar of public opinion, is it not desirable that such men should be condemned by due process of law? This can only be effected through the instrumentality of the Church Association.

If Ritualism be an evil, some means, stringent if necessary, should be adopted to repress it. The Church Association alone has sufficed hitherto to check its progress. Probably the good sense, right feeling, and love of truth and honesty inherent in the English character will ultimately stamp out what is possibly only one phase of the sensationalism of our day. But in the meantime much evil may be done, which can never be undone. We may not take much account of the wearing of vestments and burning of incense, of banners and processions. Symbolic they may be; but of what? How much is known to the juvenile, or even to the senior lay worshippers, of the alleged spiritual meaning of these symbols? All these things will amuse for the hour—this playing at religion, for it is little better —but all may pass away. But who shall calculate the evil done in the *confessional?* Let fathers, husbands, brothers look to this, if they would preserve the sacredness and purity of English homes! It is in these high interests the Church Association comes forward. For the protection of female modesty in our land this Society must continue to exist.

But there was another matter wherein the aid of the Church Association was needed, and to which it has given its attention. The Bishops were right in their estimate of the unsatisfactory state of the Ecclesiastical laws. Eminent judges and lawyers concurred in their opinion. The Church Association took up the subject, and an Ecclesiastical Reform Bill was prepared, and introduced into the House of Lords by Lord Shaftesbury. Hitherto the opponents of that measure have succeeded in interposing obstacles to its passing; but surely the Association deserves well of all true Churchmen for its endeavours to clear the Ecclesiastical Courts of anomalies, ambiguities, and enormous expenses; and place the laws Ecclesiastical on an equally sound basis with Common and Statute Law; so that cheap and sure justice may be as readily obtained in ecclesiastical as in civil and criminal causes. None can deny that in promoting the reform of our Ecclesiastical Courts the Church Association is employed on a necessary and useful work.

The efforts made for the reform of the Ecclesiastical Laws may soon be renewed; and surely it is well that an Association exists capable of rendering effective assistance.

Perhaps there may be no immediate cause for further legal action on the part of the Church Association; but who shall say how soon cases may arise absolutely requiring the aid which it alone is able, and which it is ready to afford.

Mr. Mackonochie sheltered himself from the charge of disobeying or evading the law of the land under the plea of obedience to the "Law of the Church." There is no Church whose laws Mr. Mackonochie is bound to obey save the Church of England. There never has existed since the days of the Apostles a Catholic or Universal Church competent to prescribe laws to the Christian world. The Church of England has ordained rites and ceremonies; and her laws should be binding on the conscience of all her ministers. The Lord Chancellor rightly described Mr. Mackonochie's conduct. But if he persist in his scrupulous obedience to the laws of a mythical Church, who shall say how soon he may be driven to the commission of acts which could not be tolerated.

By the judicial condemnation of all their principal innovations the whole Ritualistic body are placed in a most humiliating position; and if the moral sense were not already sadly blunted, persistency in their present illegal conduct must naturally and necessarily reduce their minds to a condition incapable of nice discrimination between right and wrong. It is difficult to conceive of men in their right mind putting forth statements with the hope they will be accepted as true without examination, simply because they are the utterances of clergymen of the Church of England. When Dr. Littledale, an acknowledged leader and reputed learned man, called the Reformers "utterly unredeemed villains," did he really know no better? When another asserts that the confessional has been "ever and only an instrument of good," does he believe his own words? When a third, who accounts himself a learned man, declares in print that Holy Communion is never called in our Formularies "The Lord's Supper," was this ignorance?

It is now said that Mr. Bennett used the word "visible" "inadvertently;" and that neither he nor anyone else holds that doctrine. If Mr. Bennett, sitting quietly in his study penning a formula on a most sacred subject, could "inadvertently" employ a term which has shocked the religious instinct of the Christian world, and which exceeds in grossness, even in the judgment of the Dean of Arches, the Romish doctrine of Transubstantiation; if he be so careless or inexact in the use of language when writing on such a subject, surely it is fully time he ceased to be a religious teacher, as well as forfeited all reputation as a theologian. But, does he and do his followers understand the meaning of the word "objective." He declares the two words mean precisely the same thing: each alike expresses what "passed through his mind when writing."

The word "visible" is intelligible; and, as employed by Mr. Bennett, well nigh blasphemous. The word "objective," in the judgment of the Bishop of St. David's, "may mean anything or nothing." Curiosity might well inquire how his followers interpret it! But how soon may such a man afford additional work for the Church Association! How soon may his language become such as shall compel the judges to pass sentence on him as a heretic!

But there is one branch of its operations to which

the Association may now devote its attention more directly than hitherto. It has been shown that without any marked efforts in that direction its influence has operated favourably in drawing into closer union the Evangelical body. The Council say well in their Annual Report for 1871 that God in the past year "has been pleased to bless their efforts to vindicate the Protestant and Evangelical character of the Church of England, and to uphold in their purity and simplicity those principles which our martyred Reformers sealed with their blood."

But they add : " The necessity of some measure for the promotion of greater unity of feeling and action among Churchmen attached to the principles of the Reformation has long forced itself upon their attention. It has for some time been their desire to take up this branch of work which from temporary circumstances had been suspended."

That the Evangelical body is much divided, has been the taunt of its enemies as well as the lament of its best members. Good men and true have stood aloof from one another on account of differences such as must exist in every large body composed of worthy men. Bad men conspire readily ; and the badness of a cause may be guaged by the readiness with which men join it : indifferent men who hold their principles, such as they are, loosely, find few obstacles to united action. But where there is real excellence there is a repulsive, as well as an attractive force in operation. While sterling worth tends to bring its possessors together, disparity of disposition and dissimilarity in habit of thought, such as must exist in every community of imperfect beings, however high the attainments, moral and intellectual, of the individual members, too often operate as a power of repulsion far stronger than is warrantable. When principles are held with a praiseworthy tenacity, that tenacity is apt to extend to opinions and purposes no way deserving the importance attached to them. The deeply conscientious man hesitates to sacrifice minor points lest he should be betrayed into the relinquishment of some principle. Good men will often have, and sometimes cherish far too dearly a favourite crotchet.

The truth of the apothegm, " Union is strength," has not been fully or practically acknowledged by the Evangelical body; and the absence of concerted action has proved a source of weakness. It usually requires a common danger to drive good men together; and in the presence of such a danger a rallying point is essential to combination. A common danger of no inconsiderable magnitude has arisen in the assault made on the Protestant character of our Church; and a satisfactory rallying point is offered in the Church Association.

It is well to realize to its full extent the danger that threatens us : that it is great who can doubt ? With a Government apparently playing into the hands of the Ultramontane priesthood, one of whom can apply no stronger term than " questionable " to a blasphemous publication, and who can laud to the skies the father of German Neology; with bishops who, whether from timidity, or excess of caution, or overstretched charity, or ill disguised sympathy, tacitly allow an unscrupulous party to continue their illegal practices and preach their anti-Scriptural doctrines; with Secularism and Infidelity rampant throughout the land ; with Rationalism within the Church, and prevalent among some bodies of Nonconformists; who can deny that Protestantism and spiritual religion are beset by many and great dangers?

The power of God alone can protect and preserve his truth, but it is ours, in dependance on that power, to " contend earnestly for the faith once delivered to the saints."

Surely, then, we should do all in our power to

strengthen the hands of the Council of the Church Association; and so co-operate in bringing about a heartier and closer union of the people of God.

This is so manifestly a work in the very spirit of the Gospel, that they who doubted or disliked the course of legal proceedings into which the Council were driven can hardly fail to acknowledge that, now at least the Church Association has got before it true and proper work. If any loyal member of the Church has doubted of the means hitherto employed " to uphold the Doctrines, Principles, and Order " of his Church, or of the wisdom and soundness of the course followed by the Council, surely he can doubt no more. No sound hearted man can be unwilling " to encourage concerted action for the advancement and progress of spiritual religion ; " and the mode of doing this now proposed by the Council of the Church Association must surely commend itself to every thoughtful Christian man.

CHAPTER V.

ITS FUTURE.

WHO may say what shall be the Future of the Church Association? Its work? Its destiny? The one may depend much on the perverseness of man : the other we know shall be determined by the Providence of God. We have seen that it stands in Its Present as a rallying point for the loyal sons of the Church of England. True-hearted men are gradually acknowledging it as a centre of union and joining its standard. They will do so more and more as they observe more clearly the signs of the times. The necessity of such a source of concentrated action will become more and more manifest as the enemy shows a bolder front, and betrays a more deadly hatred to the truth, and his inherent enmity to the God of truth. As the flood of ungodliness deluges our land, individual action will probably become less and less practicable and efficient. Each man of God may now bring the Word of Truth to bear on those immediately around him. Each faithful minister of Christ has, at present, opportunity to press home on the consciences of his flock the precious truths of the Gospel. Each is still free to preach Christ as the one and only Saviour of sinners.

But who may say how long shall last this time of comparative peace? Who can say how soon may come times when united action alone shall be possible? Who shall say for how short a space it shall be permitted the faithful servant of our Divine Master to occupy the vantage ground now held by him?

How soon may an ambitious and eccentric Minister, once the staunch defender of Established Churches, determine that the Church of England shall be no more? Is he unlikely to repeat what he has once done? Who but ONE can restrain this man, who, to the full extent of his power, has already quenched the light of truth in Ireland? How soon may he exert that same power, which he wields so haughtily and exercises so impulsively, upon the Church of this land? and, backed by Romanists, Secularists, and Liberationists, shall rob and despoil the Church, which since its reformation has for 300 years been the glory and safeguard of our country and the bulwark of Protestantism throughout the world!

And farther : who can deny the rapid progress made throughout Europe of anarchy, infidelity, and superstition, the " three unclean spirits " that have come out of the mouth of the dragon, and out of the mouth of the beast, and out of the mouth of the false prophet. Not the least rapid has been that progress in this our Protestant land ; rendering it by no means impossible that the very framework of society may soon be shattered, the throne cast down, and an infidel communism revel in the destruction of order and authority.

Who that marks these things can doubt that the " perilous times " of the last days are at hand? Notice the peculiar applicability to the present generation of some at least of the characteristics enumerated by St. Paul in 2 Tim. iii., " Men shall be lovers of their own selves, covetous, boasters, proud, blasphemers, disobedient to parents," " lovers of pleasures more than lovers of God, having a form of godliness, but denying the power thereof."

Add to these the painful sights we are called to witness among the clergy :—what departure of sons from the faith of their fathers ; what falling away of those who seemed to run well ; what compromise of principle under the false notion of conciliation ; what conformity to the world to escape the charge of singularity ; what coldness and lukewarmness under the plea of moderation ; what abstention from declaring the whole counsel of God through fear of exciting prejudice ; what sacrificing of the power of the pulpit to the adornment of the chancel and the efficiency of the choir ! Are not these things so ?   Then, if the signs of the times are thus interpreted aright ; if the word of prophecy shine on our day with other than a dim and feeble light, surely it becomes the children of God to gird up the loins of their minds !

Is not tribulation foretold for the last times ? Times of trial and temptation, possibly times of persecution ? Does not our Lord's universal command to "watch" bear in these days a peculiar force and significance ? Should not they who now fear the Lord speak very often one to another ?   Does not all around seem to impress upon true Christians the necessity of combination and concentration ?

Then who shall say that the Church Association may not be the organization designed and blessed of God for the promotion of perfect union and communion of all His people within this land ?

Our blessed Lord's prayer that all that believe on Him through the word of His servants "may be one," is still unanswered.   The Church Association may prove the honoured instrument of hastening the answer.

It may be that true-hearted Nonconformists, waiving all minor differences, shall hereafter see it to be their wisdom and their strength to become members of the Church Association.

It is now an association for bringing together the faithful sons of the Church of England ; but it may become more emphatically a Church Association for the union of all true disciples of Christ—the expression and representative in this land of that one, true, catholic, apostolic, and invisible Church, composed of the redeemed out of all nations, languages, and tongues.

How great honour, then, may await those who guide the movements of the Church Association! Even now are the members of the Council and officers had in honour of all who realize the importance of the work to which they have bent their energies. But in the future—and who shall say how soon that future may become the present?—they may be accounted as standard-bearers in the army of the Lord of Hosts!

The present and probable future form, it must be admitted, a dark picture; but it is not all dark. There are lights as well as shades—lights that reflect truth and hope. The Church and the world shall coexist to the end of the dispensation: the wheat and the tares must grow together until the harvest. The tares may vary according to soil and climate; they may at times grow unusually rank; they may resemble so nearly the blade of wheat, that men and angels fail to distinguish them; but the wheat is known to the Lord of the harvest, and not one grain shall perish. All shall ripen; all shall be gathered into the garner of the Lord. Their names were written in the book of life from the foundation of the world; and each and all shall be kept by the power of God unto salvation ready to be revealed in the last time.

Our lot is cast in troublous times; and greater troubles may be impending. "Here is the patience of the saints." It may be that we of this generation must enter the kingdom of God through much tribulation; but we know, "He is faithful that promised;" and will bring each safely through what He has ordained. Everyone shall be there on that day when the Lord makes up His jewels.

Are we cast down because truth seems to have

perished from off the earth?   It is not so : God has
reserved to Himself the seven thousand—perhaps the
seventy and seven thousand.   Christ's flock may still
be a little flock : perhaps it is so, as compared with the
numbers professing Christianity ; but "the Lord
knoweth them that are His."

Our days are days of contention ; but contention is
an evidence of life.   The quiet and the calm of the
last century was the stillness of death.   There was no
strife : because there were few or none to strive on the
Lord's side.   All slept the sleep of spiritual death.
Because evil is more apparent in our day, it does not
follow that it is more wide-spread : because it is more
manifest, it is not proved to be greater.'   That it is very
great, very deep-rooted and wide-spread cannot be
doubted.   The powers of darkness display a fearful
and unwonted activity ; perhaps because the evil One
knows that his time is short.   But it may well be
doubted whether the worst phase of existing evil is seen
in Ritualism, idolatrous as are some of its practices ;
and superstitious, not to say blasphemous, as are some
of its doctrines.   There is, indeed, abundance of folly
and puerility in its pomp and show ; but novel sights,
whether in a church or at the Crystal Palace, will
always attract a multitude ; mere lovers of music care
little whether their taste is gratified in the House of
God or at the Opera.   The religion of nature consists
in its very essence of externals : the observance of
rites and ceremonies satisfies the natural conscience ;
and therefore has always constituted the religion of the
many ; and all this Ritualism supplies.   At the same
time it is not to be doubted that as in the Romish
Church, so also among the Ritualists, there are men
conscientious and sincere.   The germ of Divine Truth
may live in the heart, though choked by the wood, hay,
and stubble with which it is overlaid.   There are many
weak men in the world ; and honesty combined with

weakness has ever proved a fruitful source of religious error : a few crafty spirits have deceived the simple multitude. Did we not know there are no assignable limits to error among such as are untaught by the Spirit of God, we might marvel at the gross, the childish, the absurd perversions of Scripture to be found in the writings of these men.

Let the people of God only recognise the duty of our day : to fight the good fight of faith : not to cherish fears within ; but to oppose manfully all enemies without, even though those enemies be of our own ecclesiastical household. Let each contend for the truth in his own little sphere, legally, charitably, scripturally ; and all in united action under the broad banner of the Church Association. Then, having fulfilled the work assigned us, we may await prayerfully, patiently, and faithfully the blessed issue : for blessed it assuredly shall be, whatever may be its nature.

www.ingramcontent.com/pod-product-compliance
Lightning Source LLC
Chambersburg PA
CBHW081527040426

42447CB00013B/3362